Moneypenny Goes Camping

Frances Usher
Illustrated by John Eastwood

Lucy and Dad were going camping with Jack and Tasha. Moneypenny was going too.

"Good, good, good," said Moneypenny. "I'll stay awake all night."

"What's that dog saying?" asked Dad.

"He says he'll be all right," said Lucy.

They were going to camp in the forest. When they got to the campsite, they put up their tent. Moneypenny helped them. Then they cooked their supper. Moneypenny helped them until it was time for bed.

"Come in the tent, Moneypenny," said Tasha, but Moneypenny wouldn't.

"I'm going to sleep outside," he said. "A lion might come – or a tiger. I'll fight them off for you. I'm very brave."

In the middle of the night, Jack woke up. Something was sitting on his chest.

"It's dark out there," said Moneypenny, "and it's started to rain. I might have a chill. Send for a vet."

"What's that dog saying?" asked Dad.

"He says he's not ill, just a bit wet," said Jack.

He tucked Moneypenny inside his sleeping bag, and they all went back to sleep.

Next day they went on a bicycle ride in the forest.

"I hope we see some ponies," said Lucy.

"I hope we see some bears," said Moneypenny.

They rode up a hill and down the other side.

They saw some animals behind the trees.

"Bears! Save me!" cried Moneypenny. "Run! Run!"

"What's that dog saying?" asked Dad.

"He says he's having fun," said Tasha.
She talked to the ponies and patted them on their
noses.

They ate their picnic under the trees. Moneypenny
helped them. Then they walked down a path
towards the little river.

"Look at those two people over there," said Lucy.
"What are they doing?"

"I think they're digging up flowers," said Jack.
"Perhaps they're going to sell them."
"That's not allowed," said Dad.
The man looked up and saw them coming.
"Quick! Let's go," he shouted.

He started to run away. The woman ran after him. Her scarf fell on the ground and she bent down to pick it up.

"Just leave it there," the man cried. "Don't worry about it."

The two of them ran off.

Moneypenny ran over to the scarf and picked it up.

"Drop it, Moneypenny," said Lucy, but Moneypenny wouldn't.

He took the scarf with him all the way back to the tent.

"You don't want that scarf," said Tasha, but Moneypenny wouldn't let go.

"Wow! Sniff this smell! It's really whiffy," he said.

"What's that dog saying?" asked Dad.

"He says he's eaten so well, he'll be asleep in a jiffy," said Jack.

Moneypenny kept the scarf with him all the time.
He took it to the camp shop. He took it to the swings.
He took it to the showers. He slept on it all night.

In the morning, they all went into town. They saw
a display about the wildlife of the forest.

"Oh, look!" said Tasha.

There were pictures of all the wild flowers.

"Aren't they beautiful?" said a man behind them.

The man was called Pete. He was a forest ranger. He helped to look after the wildlife.

"If nobody digs up the flowers," said Pete, "then everyone can enjoy them."

"We saw two people digging up the flowers," said
Lucy. "But they ran away."

"If you see them again," said Pete, "you can come
and tell me, and I'll go and talk to them."

"And I'll go with you," said Moneypenny, "and stop them running away. I'm very big and bold."

"What's that dog saying?" asked Dad.

"He says he's getting cold," said Lucy.

When they got back to the campsite that evening there was a football match. All the people from the other tents played. Moneypenny played in goal.

The ball came flying towards Moneypenny's goal. Dad got ready to shoot.

"Save it, Moneypenny! Save it," shouted Tasha, but Moneypenny wasn't there. Moneypenny had gone.

Lucy and Dad went to look for him.

"Listen! I can hear him barking," said Lucy, "but where is he?"

They looked all over the campsite. Then they saw him down by the gate.

A motorbike was just moving away.

"The people on that bike wanted to stay here tonight," said the woman at the gate, "but our campsite is full. I had to send them away."

Moneypenny tried to run after the motorbike.
He was still barking and barking.

"Let's go," he said. "Let's go and get them."

"What's that dog saying?" asked Dad.

"He says he wishes he'd met them," said Lucy.

Next morning they all went walking in the forest. Moneypenny took the scarf with him. Jack had a big map so he could tell which way to go. Moneypenny helped him.

Soon they came to a clearing in the forest. Pete the forest ranger was there, talking to people from the Camera Club. They were taking pictures of the flowers.

Suddenly, Moneypenny started to sniff the air. Then he ran away down a little path, sniffing along the ground.

"Come back, Moneypenny," called Tasha, but Moneypenny wouldn't.

He ran right down the little path, and everyone ran after him. He was still sniffing along the ground. They ran through the nettles and through the brambles. Then Moneypenny stopped very suddenly.

"Oh, look!" said Jack.

There was a motorbike nearly hidden behind the trees. The man and the woman they had seen before were under the trees, digging up flowers again. A boy from the Camera Club took their picture.

The woman looked up.

"That dog's got my scarf!" she cried.

Pete looked at Dad and Lucy, Jack, and Tasha.

"Have you seen those two people before?" he asked.

"Yes," said Dad, "we saw them digging up flowers."

"I think they're digging up flowers to sell in the town," said Pete. "That's not allowed. The police will soon stop that. The flowers must stay in the forest. I'm going over to talk to those two."

Moneypenny stayed by the motorbike just in case they tried to run away again.

"It's our last day in the forest," said Jack. "We have to go home tomorrow."

"That's sad," said Tasha. "I know! Let's have a party at the campsite tonight."

"Good, good, good," said Moneypenny. "I shall sing a song. It will be a treat for everyone."

"What's that dog saying?" asked Dad.

"He says we'll need a seat for everyone," said Lucy, and she gave Moneypenny a great big hug.